The Whale Who Swam Through Time

A 200-Year Journey in the Arctic

Written by **Alex Boersma** and **Nick Pyenson**

Roaring Brook Press • New York

Illustrated by **Alex Boersma**

About 200 years ago . . .

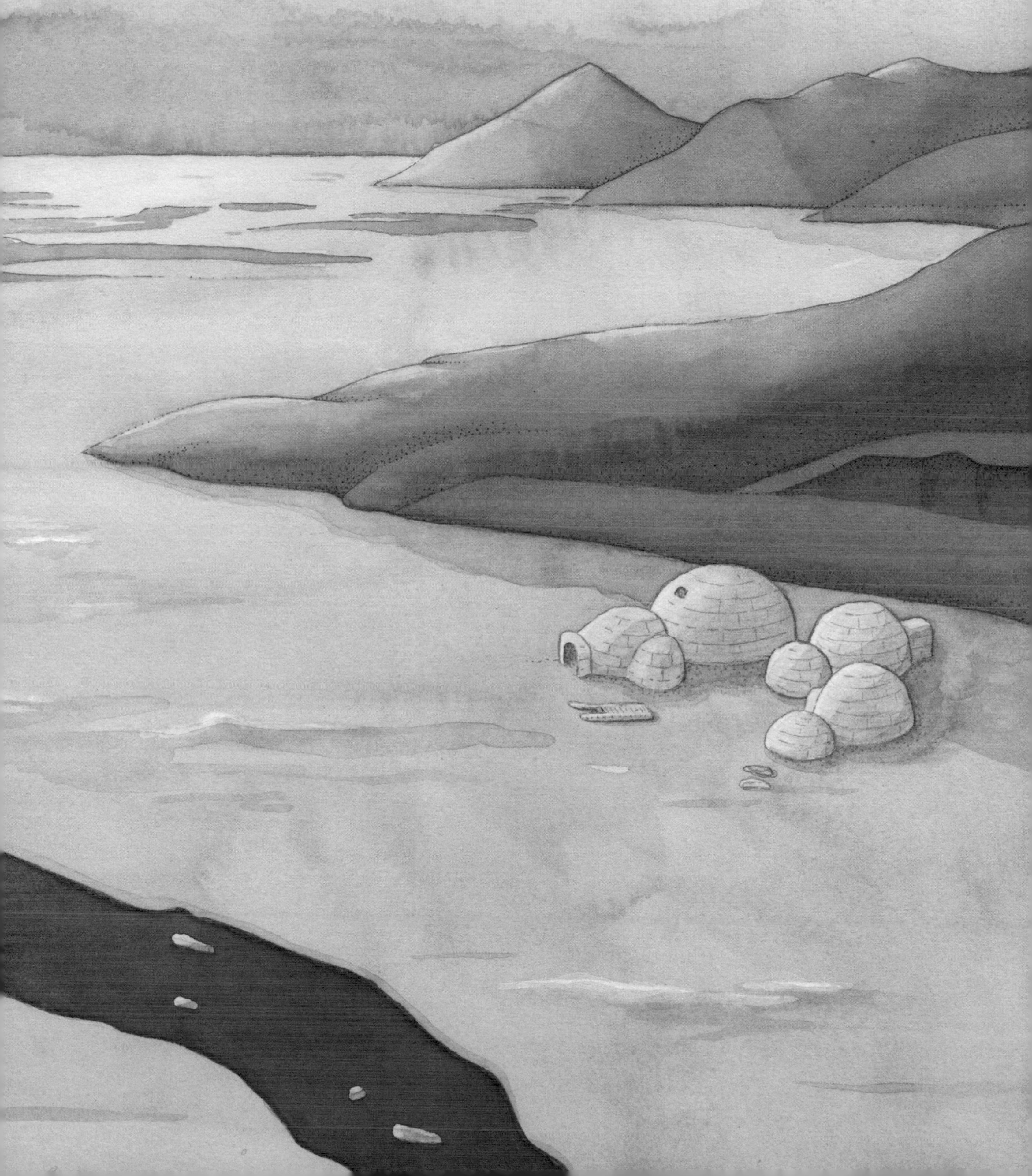

This is a story about a whale who will live a very, very long time.

She's not just any kind of whale but a bowhead whale—the longest-living mammal in the world. Bowheads are one of the few species of whales that live their whole lives in and around the Arctic.

At this moment, she rests with her mother in the quiet, cold water. Occasionally, they encounter boats: some small and paddled, and others much bigger with many sails.

The biggest ones come from half a world away, seeking a sea passage connecting the Atlantic to the Pacific. The whale finds their large forms peculiar, but they seem harmless.

The whale is just a calf, a bit longer than a rowboat. Within the year, she'll leave her mother and set off on her own. But before then, she has some important bowhead skills to learn. Her mother shows her how to use her curved snout to break through thick sea ice with a thundering

POW!

No longer nursing from her mother, the whale must learn how to feed herself. Instead of teeth she has baleen: two walls of thick, long bristles on each side of her mouth. She uses her baleen to comb through the water, filtering out tiny critters to eat.

Her favorites are copepods, which drift around
the Arctic waters in dense orange clouds.

As the years pass, she eats *more*, *more*, and *MORE*.

And she grows

bigger,

and BIGGER,

Now, almost three times longer and twenty-five years old, she is finally fully grown. The whale swims alone through the huge, open ocean.

As big as she is, it still makes her feel small.

About 150 years ago . . .

Each spring the sea ice retreats, and the whale migrates from open waters to a cozy bay.

She calls to her calf—the fifth one she's had—and the sound travels easily in the calm water.

Other kinds of whales spend their entire lives in communities, swimming, feeding, and singing together. Bowheads make their own way. They may travel with other bowheads during the migration, but they don't stay together long.

During the voyage, the whale's blubber helps her float
and store energy to nurse her calf.

But her blubber also makes her a target for whalers,
who want to turn it into oil and food.

They arrive in ships trailing black smoke,
their engines filling the water with a

RUMMMBLEEEEE

It's louder than any noise the whale has ever heard, but she doesn't yet
know to avoid the unfamiliar sound—and the ships that make it.

The whalers spot the whale and calf, and the crew launches rowboats to follow them.

A man aims and shoots a harpoon at the whale's back . . .

. . . and narrowly misses.

Alarmed, the whale and her calf dive

deep,

deep,

deep

down, until the awful rumbling of the ship fades into the distance.

About 50 years ago . . .

The whale has lived for over a hundred years. Even so, she still has many decades ahead of her.

The whalers left long ago. But harpoons have been traded for massive oil drills, creating a new danger for the whale—the Arctic is getting noisier.

Noisier and busier!

The **PING** of a submarine's sonar.

The **CLANG** of an oil rig's machinery.

The **ROAR** of a cargo ship's propeller.

Now the ships aren't just at the surface but below too. Submarines ply the ocean floor. Underwater, sound travels for many miles. Gone are the days of a quiet sea.

In fact, all this noise makes it hard for her to hear her grandchildren. She can barely make out their voices, and she fears she'll never hear them again.

Today . . .

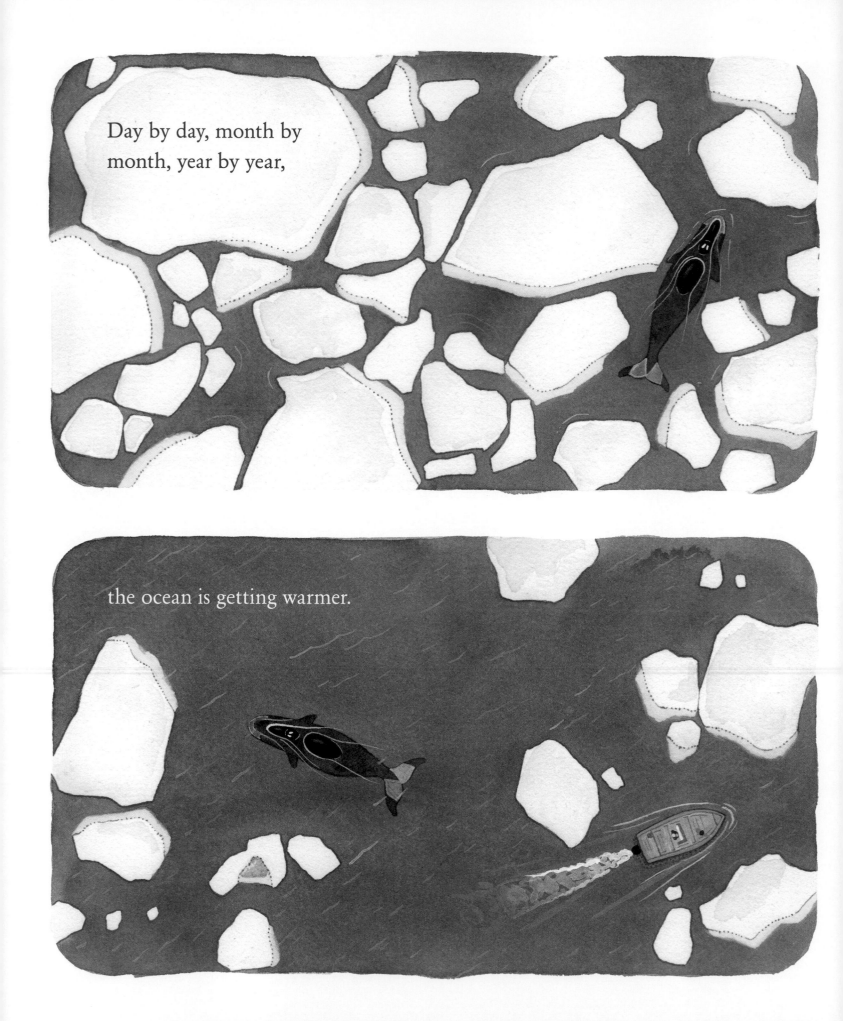

Day by day, month by month, year by year,

the ocean is getting warmer.

The whale is starting to notice less and less sea ice
roofing her world.

This new world brings new threats.

Less ice means more open ocean, and more ships with propeller blades that move too fast for whales to outswim.

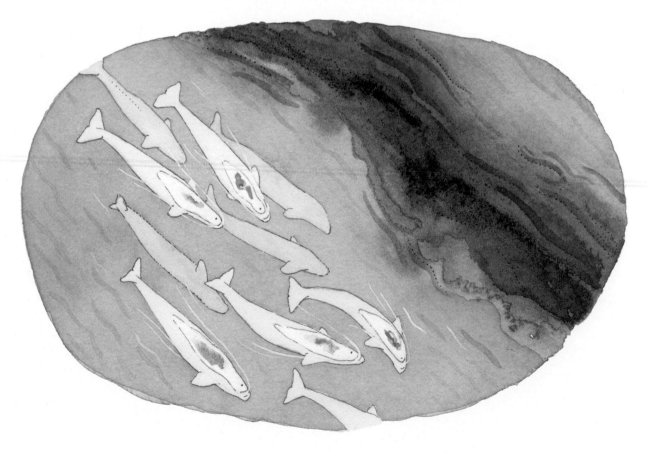

More ships also mean more oil spills.

More plastics litter the ocean, looking like food but causing harm.

And more fishing lines tangle around the flukes and flippers of whales.
There's never been more peril or more people.

Not all the changes are bad, though. A warmer Arctic brings more food and new whales! Most are friendly . . .

. . . but some are best avoided.

The whale remembers when the world was calm. But the Arctic is changing, faster and faster.

She struggles to imagine what the world will be like for her
great-grandchildren, 200 more years into a murky future.

But bowhead whales are used to swimming through uncertain waters.

AUTHORS' NOTE

Bowhead whales can live for over 200 years. When you live for that long, what is it like to see the world change around you? That question was the starting point for this book.

There's no way for us to really know what it's like to be a bowhead whale. They live their long lives so differently from ours: in a vast ocean, traveling huge distances, chasing food with giant mouths, and navigating their world by sound. Nevertheless, we wanted to take the reader along on a bowhead's two-century journey by focusing on moments of major change in her surroundings—and there have been many changes in the Arctic, especially in the last few centuries. While this story is rooted in history and biology, telling it requires a bit of imagination. We'll never understand how bowheads experience time, or how they perceive or feel about the changes in their environment, but we hope that this book helps you to both imagine how other creatures exist in this world and consider how our actions impact them.

The bowheads' long lifespan isn't the only aspect that strains our imagination. The changes in the Arctic that our whale experiences—increases in shipping traffic, oil drilling, reduced sea ice—are just a small part of the larger, global story of human activity driving climate change. Even remote parts of the world aren't immune to the effects. We think that learning how humans have changed a bowhead whale's world empowers readers young and old—and helps us become better ancestors.

How do we know bowheads can live two centuries?

Indigenous peoples of the Arctic were the first to suggest that bowheads live a very long time. The Iñupiat, who live in Alaska, sometimes describe bowheads as living as long as "two human lifetimes." By the late twentieth century, researchers had evidence for this idea when parts of nineteenth-century hunting tools were found in the long-healed scars of bowhead whales, implying that the whales were well over a hundred years old when they were killed. Later, scientists studying the longevity of bowheads measured the proportions of proteins inside the eyeballs of bowheads that had been killed by Indigenous hunters. When the scientists plotted the bowhead data with those from other mammals, their calculations showed that bowheads can live over 200 years! However, there is still a lot we don't understand about the long lives of bowheads. *How* do they manage to live so long, and *why?*

How do bowheads feed and grow?

Bowheads eat a lot differently than we do—for starters, they don't have any teeth! Instead, they have baleen—long, flexible plates of keratin (the stuff that makes your fingernails and hair) that hang from the roof of their mouths. Bowheads use their baleen to strain thousands and thousands of tiny critters out of the water to eat, which is why they are called filter feeders. While some filter-feeding whales such as

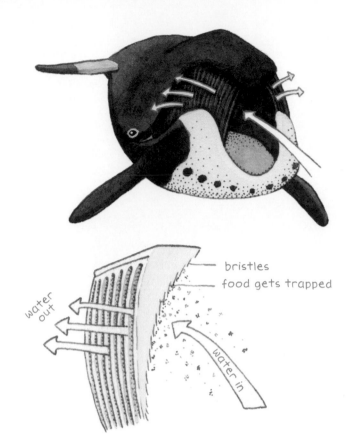

bristles
food gets trapped
water out
water in

humpbacks and blue whales feed by gulping water and prey in a single lunge, bowheads filter-feed by keeping their mouths open as they swim through swarms of their prey. Bowheads prefer to dine on copepods, tiny crustaceans the size of watermelon seeds. Sometimes, bowheads will form a tight line called an echelon (EH-shuh-lon), where they swim staggered to the left or right, nose to tail, so that every whale in the group scoops up food.

Bowheads mature a bit like we do. It takes them about 20 years or so to reach adulthood and start to have their own offspring. Once they are grown, they can weigh as much 100 tons and stretch 60 feet in length. Many other filter-feeding whales grow much faster, in a quarter or fifth of that time—we don't know why. Does it have to do with living all year round in the Arctic? Or their very large body size? Or maybe it's something in their DNA?

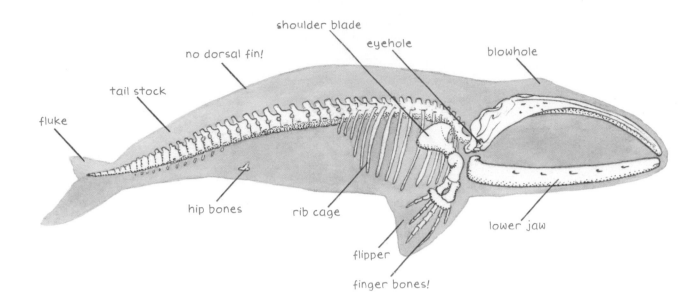

shoulder blade

no dorsal fin!

eyehole

blowhole

tail stock

fluke

hip bones

rib cage

lower jaw

flipper

finger bones!

How do bowheads communicate?

Bowheads are very vocal. They moan in long howls, groan in echoing puffs, and trill in rubbery staccatos. Scientists who have studied this wide of variety of whalesong found that it changes all the time—bowheads sing different songs year to year, and season to season, during days of full sun in the summer to the daylong darkness of the winter. Some will even sing every hour of the day! No one has yet figured out why bowheads constantly change their tune.

Where do bowheads live?

Bowheads, belugas, and narwhals are the only three whale species that spend their entire lives in the Arctic. Over time, barriers such as land and thick sea ice have separated the world's bowheads into four different populations. The East Arctic–West Greenland population (to which we imagined our bowhead

protagonist belonging) migrates away from open water in the spring to spend the summer in the sheltered waters of western Baffin Bay, northern Foxe Basin, and northwestern Hudson Bay. In the fall, as the ice grows thick and impenetrable near the shore, they migrate back to the looser pack ice of the open ocean for the winter.

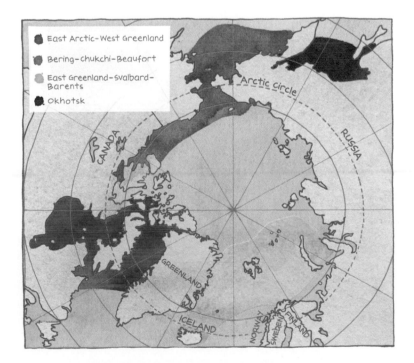

East Arctic–West Greenland

Bering–Chukchi–Beaufort

East Greenland–Svalbard–Barents

Okhotsk

Arctic Circle

CANADA

RUSSIA

GREENLAND

ICELAND

NORWAY SWEDEN FINLAND

What currently threatens bowheads?

It's not easy being a bowhead, especially right now. Humans are encroaching more and more on the Arctic, which is making the bowhead world busier, louder, and more dangerous. Like many other whales, bowheads don't move as fast as enormous cargo and cruise ships, which means that these ships mistakenly strike whales that can't get out of the way. More ships in uncharted waters also mean more chances for accidents and oil spills, which would be hard to clean up in the remote Arctic. Underwater, ships can be noisy, and so are the tools that humans use to find oil beneath the seafloor, which makes it hard for bowheads and other marine animals that navigate and communicate by sound. Disappearing ice and warmer seasons might boost bowhead numbers by increasing the amount of food they can find, but it also might have unforeseen consequences as well, such as opening the Arctic to predators such as killer whales.

Scientists still have many unanswered questions about the lives of bowhead whales. Why do they live so long? How do they hear so well? What can humans do to keep them safe as the oceans get warmer? Maybe *you* will find the answers!

Historical Notes on Inuit Peoples in the Arctic

Indigenous peoples have thrived in the Arctic for thousands of years. Today, their descendants

live in every Arctic nation except for Iceland. The first Arctic peoples entered North America across the Bering Strait over 13,000 years ago. At the time, sea level was lower, permitting an easier crossing on a land bridge called Beringia, stretching between what is now northeastern Russia and western Alaska. DNA evidence points to waves of migrations from Beringia, although some of these migrations were separated by thousands of years and did not overlap. The archaeological evidence shows that different people developed sophisticated tools for their subsistence cultures, including ways to herd, fish, navigate the seas, and hunt whales. For the bowhead whale in this book, we imagined that she might have interacted with any of the Arctic Indigenous peoples of North America, including Aleut, Yupik, and Inuit (Iñupiat) in Alaska; Inuit